Brian & Rhonda Weaver
you have been great friends,
Godly examples and such
helpful neighbours

James

By Their Fruit You Will Know Them

Other Titles in the Book by Book Video Bible Study Series:

GENESIS
Video Bible Studies with Richard Bewes, Paul Blackham and special guest Anne Graham-Lotz.
Accompanying Study Guide by Paul Blackham

EXODUS
Video Bible Studies with Richard Bewes, Paul Blackham and special guest Joseph Steinberg.
Accompanying Study Guide by Paul Blackham

PSALMS 20–29
Video Bible Studies with Richard Bewes, Paul Blackham and special guest Stephen Lungu.
Accompanying Study Guide by Paul Blackham

GALATIANS
Video Bible Studies with Richard Bewes, Paul Blackham and special guest Jonathan Edwards.
Accompanying Study Guide by Paul Blackham

JONAH
Video Bible Studies with Richard Bewes, Paul Blackham and special guest George Verwer.
Accompanying Study Guide by Paul Blackham

1 PETER
Video Bible Studies with Richard Bewes, Paul Blackham and special guest Don Carson.
Accompanying Study Guide by Paul Blackham

THE GOSPEL OF JOHN
Video Bible Studies with Richard Bewes, Paul Blackham and special guest Anne Graham-Lotz.
Accompanying Study Guide by Paul Blackham

1 & 2 THESSALONIANS
Video Bible Studies with Richard Bewes, Paul Blackham and special guest Rico Tice.
Accompanying Study Guide by Paul Blackham

Coming Soon...

2 TIMOTHY
Video Bible Studies with Richard Bewes, Paul Blackham and special guest Vaughan Roberts.
Accompanying Study Guide by Paul Blackham

James

By Their Fruit You Will Know Them

Authentic

09 08 07 06 05 04 03 7 6 5 4 3 2 1

First published in 2004 by Authentic Media
9 Holdom Avenue, Bletchley, Milton Keynes, MK1 1QR, UK
and
P.O. Box 1047, Waynesboro, GA 30830–2047, USA

Website: www.authenticmedia.co.uk

British Library Cataloguing in Publication Data
A catalogue record for this book is available from the British Library

ISBN 1–85078–570–8

Cover Design by Diane Bainbridge
Typeset by WestKey Ltd, Falmouth, Cornwall
Print Management by Adare Carwin

Contents

How To Use This Book

BOOK BY BOOK is a video-based Bible Study resource with linked Bible Study questions and a mini-commentary, provided in this Study Guide by the Rev'd Dr Paul Blackham. It has been designed principally for use in small groups, but can also be used for personal study or larger group situations.

Structure of Video and Study Guide:

There is a strong link between the video-based Bible discussions and the written Study Guide to help group discussion and study. Key features provided by the studies are as follows:

- There are 6 x programmes on the video.
- Each programme is 15 minutes long.
- The on-screen host is Richard Bewes, with co-host Paul Blackham. A specially invited guest joins them in the Bible discussions.
- Notes from the video-based discussions are printed at the start of each section of the Study Guides.
- In the Study Guide, there are also Bible Study questions on a selected portion of the text covered in each session. These focus on one short Biblical passage in greater detail.
- There is no 'answer guide' to the questions in the Study Guide – although clearly answers (and applications for daily living as Christians) are provided to questions posed during the on-screen discussions. Answers may also be found in the Further Notes at the back of the Guide.
- The Daily Readings after each Bible Study are intended to give the reader a broader picture of what is going on in each part of the Bible covered in a session.
- There are more detailed notes on each session at the back of the Study Guide. These will be of great help to leaders or anyone wanting to learn more about the particular book of the Bible. (This could also be used in isolation from the on-screen discussions as a mini-commentary.) Further questions are listed at the end of each session.

These are generally more difficult and are possibly of most use to those who would like to study the relevant passages in more detail.

Structure of Group Session:

Please note – the material has been designed in such a way that there is no need for a specially trained leader in order to be able to use the material.

Preparation

- We would highly recommend that each group member reads the relevant Bible passage prior to your discussion.
- Timing: we estimate that the study session will take about 1 hour. Given the volume of material you may even choose to take two weeks per study – using the notes linked to the video discussions for one week and the Bible Study questions for the next.
- Use of the video programme: for many, simply watching the discussion of the Bible passage may in itself be a wonderful encouragement and learning tool, and your study session may be limited to discussion on this alone. It is entirely up to your group as to whether you watch the on-screen study before or after your own group Bible Study on the passage.
- Prayer: you may want to include personal applications which arise from the discussions in your group prayer time.

Some introductory thoughts from Paul Blackham:

Thousands of small groups are starting up all over the world – but what is going to sustain them? It has to be the Bible. However, so often people don't quite know what to do with small groups. Meeting together, sharing testimonies and experiences or the odd Bible verse is ultimately too sparse a diet to sustain people's spiritual needs in the long run and really help them to grow.

What is needed is confidence in the Bible, and the ability to be able to go to a book of the Bible rather than just an isolated verse. Each book of the Bible was written with a purpose, and it is only really as we digest it as a book that we understand the real message, purpose, direction, storyline and characters.

It's a lot easier than people often think. You might think, "Oh, I can't manage a whole book of the Bible", but what we're trying to do in BOOK BY BOOK is to break it down and show that actually it's easy.

The Bible was written not for specialists, not for academics – it was written for the regular believers, down the ages.

Introduction

The book of James challenges us with the most basic and essential realities of life, driving us to face up to the truth about following Jesus the Messiah. James gives us the truth without ornament. He cuts through the kinds of excuses and delusions we cloud ourselves with. It often seems that people speak of 'faith' as if it were a matter of vague and dreamy ideas. People sometimes imagine that a mere intellectual assent to propositions within the Creed is the same as genuine faith in Jesus. As we study James we will find all such empty notions of 'faith' destroyed.

Unlike many New Testament letters, we know very little about the background of this letter. It isn't addressed to a particular church in a city like Paul's letters to the Galatians, Romans, Corinthians, etc. We don't know the date of the letter because there are no historical references.

It is also not absolutely certain which James actually wrote this letter, because he says so little about himself. He begins by describing himself as 'a servant of God and the Lord Jesus Christ', without giving us any specific job description for himself. However, the James that we meet in the book of Acts and in the letters of Paul seems to fit the bill exactly.

In the book of Acts we see the leading role that James had in the Jerusalem Church. He had enjoyed a personal appearance from Jesus after His resurrection (1 Corinthians 15:7). Most fascinating of all we see in Galatians 1:19 that Paul refers to James as the brother of the Lord. If James had grown up in the same household as Jesus and enjoyed His company and Bible study for so many years, we would expect him to be a leader in that early expansion of the Church. What an amazing childhood they must have enjoyed together!

Sometimes people have wondered just how 'Christian' the book of James is because Jesus is only mentioned explicitly in 1:1 and 2:1. However, as we understand the book in a more thorough way we see that Jesus is present at every point. He is the source of all that James teaches. The connection between the teaching of James and the teaching of Jesus is so strong that the letter only makes sense when we have the teaching of Jesus alongside the text of James' letter.

> "In the epistle of James the Holy Spirit has given the Church a commentary on Jesus' Sermon on the Mount and Sermon on the Plain, a commentary that is rich in applications for daily life."[1]

For this reason we have chosen to set the relevant teaching of Jesus at the beginning of each section of the notes (at the back of this Study Guide) so that we can see for ourselves how the brother of Jesus was so saturated with His teaching. Here is a table taken from the website **thechristian.org** showing the close parallels between the book of James and Jesus' Sermon on the Mount.

[1] George Stulac, *James*, (IVP, Leicester, 1993) page 34

	James	Matthew		James	Matthew
Inherit the kingdom	1:4	5:48	Righteousness	2:14–26	5:17–22
Perfect	1:12	7:13–14	Good works	2:18; 3:13	5:14–16
Crown of Life	1:22–26	7:24–27	Teachers	3:1	5:19–20
Hearing and doing	1:5,17	7:9–11	Speech	3:2–12	5:22
Father giving	1:5–8	7:7–11	Knowing by fruit	3:10–12	7:16–20
Prayer	1:5–8	7:7–11	Grapes and figs	3:12	7:16
Lusts and pleasures	1:13–15; 4:1–5	5:27–32	Kingdom disposition	3:13–18	5:3–12
Good gifts through prayer	1:17	7:11	Meekness	3:13	5:5
Anger	1:20	5:22	Peacemakers	3:17–18	5:9
The Law	1:25	5:17–19	Asking and receiving	4:3	7:8
Religious deception	1:16,22, 26–27	7:21–23	God and the world	4:4	6:24
Purity	1:27; 3:17; 4:8	5:8	Mourning	4:9–10	5:4
The rich	1:9–11; 5:1–6	6:19–34	Pride	4:6–10	6:1–6
Temptation	1:13	6:13	The future	4:13–17	6:25–34
The poor	2:5	5:3	Judging	4:11–12	7:1–2
Heirs of the kingdom	2:5	5:3–10	One day at a time	4:13–16	6:25
Love	2:8	5:43–48	Riches	5:2ff	6:19
The royal Law	2:8	7:12	The Lord judging	5:7–9	7:22f
Keeping the whole Law	2:10	5:17–19	Persecution	5:10–11	5:11–12
Adultery	2:10–11	5:27	Oaths	5:12	5:34ff
Mercy	2:13	5:7	Yes, Yes and No, No	5:12	5:37
Forgiveness	2:13	5:7	Forgiveness	5:15–16	6:12–15
Judgement	2:13	7:2	Restoring a brother	5:19–20	5:23–26

Video Notes

Session 1

James 1:1–18
The Testing of Your Faith

The following are questions featured in the video which accompanies this Study Guide. If you wish to, you or your group can use them to recap on what you have been watching. Following this, there is a Bible study on a section of the passage covered by this session which can be used instead or additionally.

1. Scattered 1:1

What do we know about the author of the book of James, and when this book was written?

Who was this letter written to?

2. Tested 1:2–4

We all face trials and difficult situations that can sometimes leave us feeling abandoned by God, or can really shake our faith. What does James have to say to us when we feel we are in such a situation?

3. Believing 1:5–12

When we ask for wisdom from the Father, verse 6 says we must believe and not doubt. What kind of doubting is James talking about? How can we ensure that our faith is strong enough to receive the wisdom that we ask for?

What does James have to say about poverty and wealth in verses 9–11?

4. Tempted 1:13–18

What two different reactions to trials does James outline for us in verses 12–15?

Bible Study 1

James 1:2–18

- What is the joy of trials, verse 2? Can you think of some other Bible passages that help tell us more about this joy? (Some examples are Matthew 5:10–12, and 1 Peter 1:6–7)
- James outlines two reactions to trials – one positive (verses 2–5) and one negative (verses 13–15). What are the characteristics of each? How can we encourage each other to react in the right way?
- In what ways can we see in verses 6–8 that the person who doubts is not actually a Christian?
- This means that the promises of verse 5 are for all Christians at all times. What do we learn about our Lord from this verse? How can taking these promises seriously transform our lives?
- What things do we so easily blame God with when we suffer trials? From verses 12–13 and verse 17, what should our correct view of the Lord be during these times?
- The 'success' of our faith depends on the object of our faith, not on how much faith we have (see Jesus' teaching in Matthew 17:20). How then can we be sure that our faith will produce the things promised to us in this passage?
- What things have we learnt from this study? What positive actions can we take in the coming week to put these things into practice?

Daily Readings

Day 1:	James 1:1–18
Day 2:	Matthew 5:10–12, 7:7–11, 6:19–24
Day 3:	Genesis chapter 49
Day 4:	Acts 15:1–21
Day 5:	1 Peter 1:3–12
Day 6:	Matthew 19:16–30
Day 7:	Revelation 2:8–11

Session 2

James 1:19–2:13
Doers of the Word

The following are the questions featured in the video which accompanies this Study Guide. If you wish to, you or your group can use them to recap on what you have been watching. Following this, there is a Bible study on a section of the passage covered by this session which can be used instead or additionally.

1. Quick to Listen, Slow to Speak 1:19–20

How closely does James' teaching tie in with that of Jesus?

2. Do What the Word Says 1:21–27

In verse 22, James goes so far as to say that merely listening to the Word rather than living it out is 'deceiving ourselves'. How is that?

What, according to James at the end of chapter 1, is 'true religion' and why?

3. Don't Show Favouritism 2:1–7

What challenge does this passage about favouritism hold for us today? Why is favouritism so incompatible with faith in Jesus?

4. The Law That Gives Freedom 2:8–13

James goes on to comment on the Law of the Old Testament, and how showing favouritism breaks the Law. Why mention the Law here? What does James think of it?

Looking at verse 13, how much mercy does a person have to show before they receive mercy on Judgment Day?

Bible Study 2

James 1:19–25

- What is the link between verses 19 and 20?
- How is Jesus our model for verses 19–20? Think of Mark 15:4–5. Why did Jesus behave in this way?
- We cannot get rid of 'moral filth' and 'evil' (verse 21) by our own efforts. What does this verse say should happen for us to be free of sin?
- In what way do we deceive ourselves by listening to the Bible and not doing what it says?
- How does the illustration in verses 23–25 help us understand this further?
- Is a 'mirror' a good way of thinking about the Bible? What do we do if we see something in the mirror that looks awful?
- James describes the Hebrew (Old Testament) Scriptures as 'the perfect law that gives freedom' (verse 25). Are we guilty of ignoring the Old Testament Scriptures in our Bible readings? How can we see them as giving us freedom? (See Psalm 119:32)

Daily Readings

Day 1: James 1:19–2:13

Day 2: Matthew 5:21–22, 7:24–27, 12:33–37

Day 3: 1 Peter chapter 2

Day 4: Psalm 119:1–24

Day 5: Deuteronomy chapter 6

Day 6: Romans 8:1–17

Day 7: Galatians chapter 5

Session 3

James 2:14–26
Faith Without Works is Dead

The following are questions featured in the video which accompanies this Study Guide. If you wish to, you or your group can use them to recap on what you have been watching. Following this, there is a Bible study on a section of the passage covered by this session which can be used instead or additionally.

1. Faith by Itself is Dead 2:14–19

'Faith by itself, if it is not accompanied by action, is dead' (verse 17). Should this alarm us?

Is it enough to believe in God? Would a person who believes in God be saved?

How does James' teaching on faith and works compare with that of the apostle Paul? Are they in agreement?

2. Abraham's Faith and Works 2:20–23

How does the reference to Abraham help teach us about this relationship between faith and works?

3. Not by Faith Alone 2:24–26

Similarly, how does the example of Rahab explain things further? Why choose Rahab?

The Scriptures are packed with examples of believers with a living faith. Can we summarize what we have learnt in this section about faith shown through works?

Bible Study 3

James 2:14–26

- What kind of 'faith' has no deeds?
- Culture today often encourages us to think of our beliefs as a very personal and private thing. What would James have to say about that?
- How can we be sure that our deeds display what we believe to those around us? How do we make sure that we are not seen as simply 'good people'?
- Look at verse 19. What do demons believe about God? What is the difference between that, and what we as Christians believe? Are we incorporating those vital beliefs into our evangelism?
- What did Abraham's deeds prove? (verses 21–24) Would it have been possible for him to have been saved through deeds alone, or faith alone?
- Abraham is often called the 'father of the faith'. How else is he our example in the way faith and deeds work together? See Hebrews 11:8–12.
- Can you sum up the message of this passage in one sentence? How will this impact your daily life?

Daily Readings

Day 1: James 2:14–26

Day 2: Matthew 7:16–24, 5:16–20, 23:23–26

Day 3: Genesis 22:1–19

Day 4: Joshua chapter 2 and 6:20–25

Day 5: Romans 3:21–4:5

Day 6: Hebrews 11:1–19

Day 7: Hebrews 11:20–40

Session 4

James 3:1–17
No Man Can Tame the Tongue

The following are questions featured in the video which accompanies this Study Guide. If you wish to, you or your group can use them to recap on what you have been watching. Following this, there is a Bible study on a section of the passage covered by this session which can be used instead or additionally.

1. A Warning to Teachers 3:1–8

We begin chapter three with what is perhaps a surprising verse. What is the message for those who teach?

How important are our words? How powerful is the tongue?

What is the 'fire' of the tongue, verse 6? How can it be controlled?

2. Out of the Same Mouth 3:9–12

What is the impossible contradiction of our tongues in verses 9–12?

3. Who is Wise among You? 3:13–17

In verse 13, James makes a fresh challenge. Who is this challenge specifically for, and why?

How do we know when a person has true wisdom, verses 17–18?

Bible Study 4

James 3:2-12

- The word 'perfect' in verse 2 is the same Greek word as is used for 'mature and complete' in 1:4. What part does our speech play in the process of becoming spiritually mature?
- Look at what Jesus says about speech in Matthew 12:34. What else does our speech reveal about us? How does this fit in with James' teaching in verse 2 of our passage?
- What do the examples in verses 3–5 tell us about the tongue? Can you identify with these things?
- Verses 6–8 are so strong. Why is it that this issue of the tongue and speech is so important? Think perhaps of the great contrast between our speech and the speech of the Lord God. (Remember Genesis 1:3, John 1:1)
- Look at verses 9–12. Outline the two different extremes used to describe what the tongue is capable of. How different are they?
- It is clear that James is talking about the unbeliever as the person who curses, and the Christian as the person who blesses. However, we all know that despite being a 'new creation' in the Lord, we still turn back to our old wicked ways. When we as Christians use our tongues to curse, what are we doing? Who are we following?
- How has this study made us think about our speech? What can we do about it?

Daily Readings

Day 1: James 3:1–17

Day 2: Matthew 7:16–21; 12:33–37; 15:8–20

Day 3: Psalm 33

Day 4: Proverbs chapter 8

Day 5: 1 Corinthians 1:18–2:16

Day 6: 1 Kings chapter 3

Day 7: Colossians chapter 3

Session 5

James 3:18–4:17
Humble Yourselves before the Lord

The following are questions featured in the video which accompanies this Study Guide. If you wish to, you or your group can use them to recap on what you have been watching. Following this, there is a Bible study on a section of the passage covered by this session which can be used instead or additionally.

1. Peace and Strife 3:18–4:3

Why are there fights and arguments in the Church family?

How does James help us understand the issue of 'unanswered prayers' in 4:3?

2. God versus the World and the Devil 4:4–10

Why does James suddenly call his readers 'adulterous people' in verse 4?

What encouragements are there here for the Christian life? (verses 6–8)

3. All Such Boasting is Evil 4:11–17

In what way is slander breaking the Law, verse 11?

Does James forbid any forward planning in verses 13–17?

Bible Study 5

James 4:1–10

- What perspective does James put on fights within the Church family? Is this how we see them?
- What does this mean for us if we are involved in such a quarrel? What are we to do about it?
- We often get upset if our prayers go 'unanswered'. What do verses 2–3 teach us about prayer? (See also 5:16–18 and 1:13–17)
- Why does James call his readers 'you adulterous people' in verse 4? What kind of adultery and marriage is he talking about?
- 'Envy' would come under the list of sinful desires that cause fights in verse 1. How then is it possible for the Holy Spirit to be envious, verse 5? What kind of jealousy is this? (See Exodus 20:5, 34:14)
- How do the ideas of marriage, adultery or envy help us look on our personal relationship with the Lord Jesus? Does it make you want to change your attitude or actions towards Him?
- What is the Lord's response to our 'adultery' with the world, verse 6?
- What are some of the ways we can grow closer to the Lord, as given in verses 6–10?

Daily Readings

Day 1: James 3:18–4:17

Day 2: Matthew 5:1–9; 5:21–24 and Luke 18:9–14

Day 3: Philippians 2:1–18

Day 4: Isaiah chapter 57

Day 5: Hosea chapter 11

Day 6: Revelation chapter 21

Day 7: Matthew 18:15–35

Session 6

James 5:1–20
The Judge is Standing at the Door

The following are questions featured in the video which accompanies this Study Guide. If you wish to, you or your group can use them to recap on what you have been watching. Following this, there is a Bible study on a section of the passage covered by this session which can be used instead or additionally.

1. Weep and Wail You Rich People 5:1–6

What do we learn about wealth and its dangers from the first part of chapter 5?

2. The Lord is Coming 5:7–12

How does James encourage us to keep our eyes fixed on the future and the great coming of Jesus?

How do the references to the Old Testament prophets encourage us here? What do we learn from them and why should we study them?

3. Praying in Faith 5:13–20

James addresses the question of illness, and praying for those who are sick. We know from experience that people are not always healed through prayer. How can we explain these verses?

What do we learn about prayer from the rest of this chapter?

What are James' concluding thoughts?

Can you sum up the teaching of the book of James? What are some of the things that stand out?

Bible Study 6

James 5:5–11

- Why does the Lord delay His return? See 2 Peter 3:8–9. How does this help us be patient?
- What is the 'valuable crop' that we as the farmer of verse 7 are waiting for?
- Why does James warn us not to grumble against each other in the light of Jesus' return, verse 9? How will we live with one another in the New Creation? (Revelation 7:13–17)
- Which Old Testament characters encourage you to be patient during suffering? When we read about their lives do we apply their lessons to our own Christian lives?
- How can we become more like Job in our own response to suffering? Look at his attitude: Job 1:20–22, 19:25–26.
- Why does James remind us that the Lord is 'full of compassion and mercy' at the end of verse 11?
- What have these studies in James taught you? What has stood out the most and changed your life? You may want to spend some time praying together that you will be able to live out these truths and help each other to do so.

Daily Readings

Day 1: James 5:1–20

Day 2: Luke 6:20–26, Matthew 5:33–37

Day 3: Matthew 6:19–34

Day 4: Acts 4:32–5:11

Day 5: 1 Kings 18:16–40

Day 6: Psalm 89:1–29

Day 7: Revelation 7:9–17

Further Notes

Session 1

James 1:1–18
The Testing of Your Faith

Key Truth: It is through trials that our relationship with Jesus is deepened and we grow to become mature believers, trusting without unbelief in the goodness of the Lord.

Jesus' Teaching:
Matthew 5:10–12 'Blessed are those who are persecuted because of righteousness, for theirs is the kingdom of heaven. Blessed are you when people insult you, persecute you and falsely say all kinds of evil against you because of Me. Rejoice and be glad, because great is your reward in heaven, for in the same way they persecuted the prophets who were before you.'
See also Matthew 7:7–11, Matthew 6:19–24, Matthew 5:48

1. Scattered 1:1

This letter is from James, but straight away we need to clear up a translation issue. The proper translation of his name is 'Jacob', and it is a strange historical peculiarity that the English name James has been chosen to represent the Greek for Jacob. We could refer to this as the letter of Jacob!

If we think in this way, the first verse would read: 'Jacob, a servant of God and of the Lord Jesus Christ, to the twelve tribes scattered among the nations: Greetings.' When we see it like this our minds are drawn to the Hebrew Scriptures, in particular Genesis 49 when Jacob blessed the twelve tribes of Israel. The letter of James is based on Jesus' teaching, and it is filled out with all kinds of references to the Hebrew Scriptures. Sometimes people have treated James' letter as a simple collection of practical tips. However, the letter is written from great theological depth and Scriptural knowledge. Its practicality is unquestioned, but its theological depth needs to be always kept in our minds.

This letter from James is addressed to 'the twelve tribes scattered among the nations'. This Hebrew Scripture language is often used to describe all those who trust in Jesus – a Jewish title for all Christians over the world.[1]

James begins his letter by emphasising that there is just one family of God in both the Old Testament and the New Testament. This letter is addressed to Israel, spread across the whole world, containing both Jews and Gentiles who trust in the Jewish Messiah.

2. Tested 1:2–4

James' statement about trials in verse 2 is quite a shock. He knew that facing opposition and suffering would be a real challenge for every Christian believer sooner or later. Whether we are suffering for the sake of the gospel, tormented by physical illness or distressed in difficult circumstances, we might well feel abandoned by the Living God unless we understand what is happening to us.

James explains that the trials we face are like fertile soil for fruitful growth. As our trust in Jesus is tested (verse 2) so our perseverance is developed. When everything is comfortable and easy, our wayward hearts tend to trust Jesus less and less. When we are under pressure, then

---

[1] Sometimes people speak as if the LORD God had two covenants, two chosen people. They imagine that the LORD has a racial choice based on fleshly genetic heritage, with its own covenant, and, on the other hand, a 'gospel' choice based on faith in Jesus. Some have even gone so far as to say that unbelieving Jews do not need evangelism! This seems to create deep Biblical problems. In Romans chapters 9–11, the apostle Paul specifically and carefully demonstrates that God's choice of Israel was never based on genetics, never based on mere Abrahamic ancestry. He shows that, to the LORD God, Israel is **always** a matter of **faith**, always open to all people regardless of genetics. There is no racial prejudice in the Living God at all. A Jewish person should be the very first to acknowledge Jesus (Romans 9:1–5; 11:24), but if they do not, they are not part of the LORD's chosen people. 'Not all who are descended from Israel are Israel' (Romans 9:6). The Jew who rejects Jesus the Jewish Messiah rejects Israel and their Jewish roots. The Gentile who trusts in Jesus is joined into Israel, grafted into the Jewish covenant (Romans 11:17–24). To treat a Gentile believer as belonging to a secondary covenant or a secondary people is just racial prejudice! The Gentile believer is fully included in Israel when they trust Jesus, even though they are a 'wild branch' rather than a Jewish 'natural branch'.

our illusions of self-dependence begin to break down and we hold onto Jesus with the kind of love and trust that is right. These times of trial then are times of growth when our relationship with Jesus is deepened. When we share in the sufferings of Jesus we are drawn closer to Him. Therefore, facing trials should be times of 'pure joy' because they are intimate times with Jesus.

James shows us a **chain of maturity**. He assumes that there is nothing we desire more than spiritual maturity, a close walk with Jesus, righteous integrity.

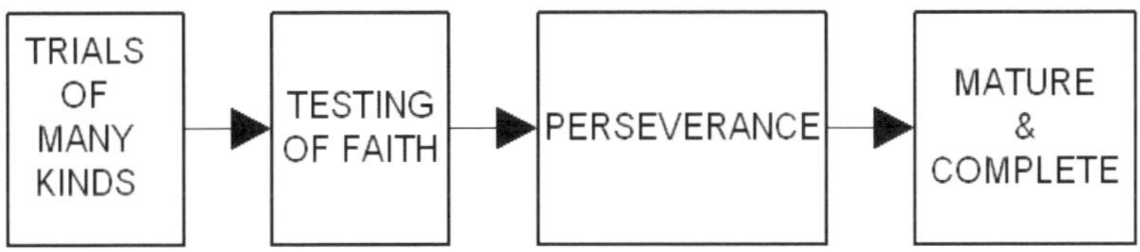

We are again taken to the teaching of Jesus. In Matthew 5:48 Jesus uses this same Greek word for completion, perfection or maturity ('teleios') to describe both God the Father and what the Christian must be. James here shows us how we can fulfil Jesus' command to be perfect. We should greet our trials with nothing but joy because they are bringing us closer to the perfection of our Father in heaven.

3. Believing 1:5–12

In these verses, James continues his teaching about the way we respond to 'trials of many kinds'. The response of genuine faith is to ask for wisdom when we are struggling. When times are difficult, we might wonder what to do, how to keep going, why it is happening, etc. We feel our lack of wisdom, and we know that we cannot develop or build up our own wisdom. We need our Father's wisdom.

Our Father generously gives wisdom to us 'without finding fault' (verse 5). We are reminded of Jesus' teaching from Matthew 7:7–11. Our Father is amazingly gracious, more generous than the most indulgent parent. He will always give us what we need if we ask Him. He won't hold grudges about our sin or refuse our request because of mistakes in our prayers. No, He is always ready to give us the wisdom that we need to move us ever closer to perfection and maturity.

So, there is never going to be a problem from our Father when we call to Him in our trials. However, there may well be a problem from our side if we do not really trust Him (verses 6–8).

Throughout his letter James is very keen to show the difference between genuine faith and 'pretend' faith. One of the main targets of the letter is the person who is 'religious' or 'nominally Christian' – the person who imagines that they are trusting Jesus when in fact they are still, deep down, trusting in their own resources and abilities.

In verse 6, James is not saying that we must work up such an intensity of rock-solid 'faith' in order to 'earn' a favourable answer. NO! James is exposing the **object** of faith – what we are trusting in. The **amount** of faith we have is not the issue. Jesus Himself taught that we need only the tiniest amount of genuine faith in Him in order to do whatever is needed (Matthew 17:5–6, 20). We rely on **Jesus**, not our own ability.

James shows us that a man who is double-minded (literally 'double-souled') does not trust in the Father at all. There is no genuine trust in their heart. Requests for wisdom from a person who does not yet trust the Father at all will not be granted. Such a person doesn't need help in Christian growth... they simply need to become a Christian!

We must remember that when James speaks of 'doubt' here, he is not speaking about **moments** of uncertainty or turmoil in the believer. The contrast here is between faith and unbelief, trust in Jesus versus trust in money or self.

In verses 9–11 James addresses one particular trial that must have been a common one for those apostolic Christians – poverty. Jesus Himself said that it was extremely difficult for a rich person to be saved, Matthew 19:21–27. James seems to say that it is extremely likely that rich people will place their trust in money rather than Jesus. The poor person is not more spiritual than the rich person, nor is it that our Father intrinsically prefers poor people to rich people, but if we are to take Jesus' words seriously then it does seem that the poor are more likely to cast themselves onto the grace and mercy of the Lord God.

The Christian facing a life of poverty should not allow their material circumstances to determine their outlook on life. Rather, they need to take pride in the exalted, wealthy position that they have in Jesus. The Christian who is wealthy should take the **same** view of life, boasting that the riches he has been given are nothing compared to the treasure of life in Jesus. James sees being rich as much as a trial as being poor.

We are not to focus on our earthly poverty or wealth, but to live for the treasure that we have in Jesus, the glorious, incorruptible **crown of life** that is ours in our resurrection future.

4. Tempted 1:13–18

Now James looks more closely at the dangers we face in our times of trial. If we are to experience the growth and maturity that the Lord offers us in trials we must be on guard against our sin.

We see the two possible reactions to the trials of many kinds: the reaction of genuine faith that leads to maturity/perfection or the reaction of unbelief that leads to sin and death.

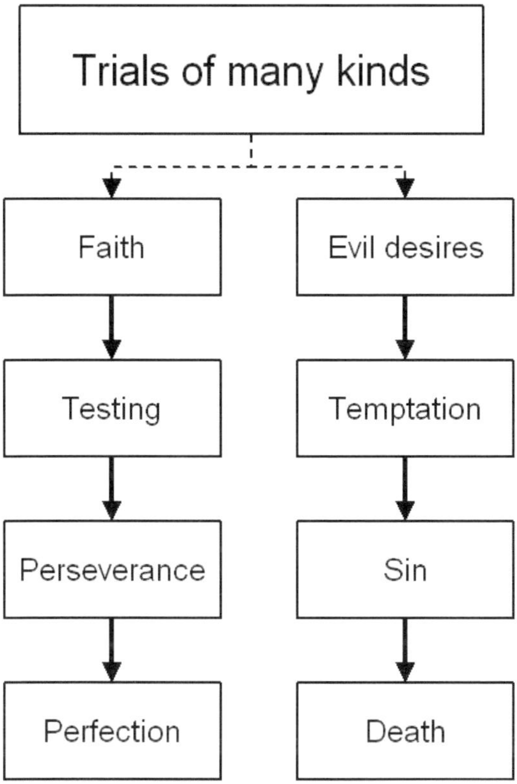

In verses 13–15 James warns us about the sinful chain that happens when trials are faced by unbelief. If instead of trusting our Father we refuse to trust in Him, then our trials are simply a time of temptation. We might feel sympathetic when a person accuses the Living God of wrong when they are going through a hard time, but such a reaction is actually dangerous. Job refused to curse the LORD God when he faced his trials, saying 'Naked I came from my mother's womb, and naked I will depart. The LORD gave and the LORD has taken away; may the name of the LORD be praised.' (Job 1:21) The Bible says about him: 'In all this, Job did not sin by charging God with wrongdoing.'

When we face trials, the danger is that we will be tempted into sin and then blame the Father for our sin. We might repay the evil done to us with evil (see Romans 12:17). We might give ourselves to the pursuit of earthly wealth in our poverty. We might commit adultery if our marriage is tested. We might commit sexual immorality when we struggle with loneliness. We might compromise with the world when it hates us and rejects us. In all these ways we might treat our trials as a temptation to sin and end up blaming the Living God for our sin.

James sternly warns us about any such reaction. The trials we face have nothing to do with the sinful temptations that may spring up from our own evil hearts. If we make sinful choices during trials, it is because of the evil desires in our hearts, not because our Father has allowed these trials to come upon us, verse 14. The Father never intends for us to respond to trials with anything other than love, trust and obedience.

Far from ever leading us towards sin, our generous, holy Father only ever gives us good things that save us from the power of sin and death. We should never wickedly imagine that the Living God is compromised between light and darkness. He appointed the heavenly witnesses of the sun, moon and stars with their constant, pure light, verses 17–18. Whether we always see their light or not, we always know that they are shining their light into the dark universe. In the Lord there is not the slightest bit of darkness (1 John 5:3). In Psalm 19 the sun's faithful daily victory over darkness is a constant witness to the glory of the LORD God over the darkness.

If evil desires give birth to sin and death, the utterly wonderful gift of the Father is the gospel which gives us birth as 'firstfruits' of creation. He gives us birth through 'the word of **truth**', which stands against the lies of verse 13. 'Firstfruits' is a term from the Hebrew Scriptures. In 1 Corinthians 15:20–23, Jesus is called the firstfruits from the dead. He is the first 'crop' of the resurrection, anticipating and guaranteeing the full future 'harvest' of all those who are in Christ. In James 1:18 we see that we are the firstfruits of the creation in that we have been given birth by the word of truth for a life free of evil desires, temptation, sin and death. The Father's purpose for the creation is shown in us. His future harvest is one of truth, goodness, sinlessness and immortality.

Further Questions

1. How many almost direct references to Jesus' teachings can you find in these verses? How does this help us to understand James?

2. Why is the title 'the twelve tribes' also used to refer to believers in Jesus from all over the world? Where else in the Bible can you find this used in such a way? How does it help us understand the Israel of the Old Testament?

3. Can you explain what the word 'firstfruits' means in the Bible?

Session 2

James 1:19–2:13
Doers of the Word

Key Truth: During times of trial, we are doers of the Word, sharing God's love practically with all in the Church family, without favouritism.

Jesus' Teaching:
Luke 6:46–49 'Why do you call Me, 'Lord, Lord,' and do not do what I say? I will show you what he is like who comes to Me and hears My words and puts them into practice. He is like a man building a house, who dug down deep and laid the foundation on rock. When a flood came, the torrent struck that house but could not shake it, because it was well built. But the one who hears My words and does not put them into practice is like a man who built a house on the ground without a foundation. The moment the torrent struck that house, it collapsed and its destruction was complete.'
See also Matthew 5:21–22, Matthew 7:24–27, Matthew 12:33–37

1. Quick to Listen, Slow to Speak 1:19–20

In session 1, we saw how James explained the two responses to trials – faith, or unbelief. He now shows us specifically how we are to act in these times of trial. For James, the way that we speak is one of the very deepest aspects of our spiritual life. A person reveals their spiritual state by their speech.

James' tough challenges are not motivated by anything but love for the Christian family. He begins with the affectionate words 'my dear brothers'.

In times of trial one of the grave dangers is that we will speak evil. James tells us what to do – we should prefer listening to speaking. He sees a close connection between the speed of our speaking and the speed of our anger. Slow to speak goes with slow to anger. When we give free reign to express our anger we are also giving free reign to our anger itself.

In 1 Peter 2:20–23, Peter explains that enduring suffering in a way pleasing to God is shown in the way that we speak during our trials. Jesus is the model for us in all this. He spoke no angry words of any kind during His terrible trial. There were no threats or curses. In fact, He spoke blessing to those who hurt Him.

2. Do What the Word Says 1:21–27

The alternative to angry words and hasty speech is to get rid of the evil and filth that lies behind it, verse 21.

But we are not able to purify ourselves. Rather, the word of truth that gave us a new birth (verse 18) is the same word that is able to cleanse us from the evil that is within us. James describes this word as 'planted' within the believer, implying that the truth of the gospel/Scripture has become part of the very life of the believer. However, there is nothing magical or automatic about this cleansing process. Our moral filth and evil can only be expunged as we **do what the word says**. The word of truth can save us from evil and angry words **only** if we actually put into practice the teaching of the Bible.[2]

It is so easy to sit and listen to excellent Bible teaching week-in and week-out, but it is quite a different matter to practice what we learn from the Bible week-in and week-out. It is all too common to confuse a love of **listening** to the Bible with a love of **obeying** the Bible. Biblical orthodoxy is defined by **doing** what the Bible says, not just with confessing what the Bible teaches. This is why James warns us in verse 22 that merely **listening** to the word is so dangerous in terms of self-deception.

In verses 23–25 James contrasts two kinds of looking. James thinks of the quickest kind of looking we come across in day-to-day life. He describes a man who glances at himself in the mirror on his way out in the morning. It is a quick look, with no need for detailed examination or study. If we look at the Bible in **that** way we will get no benefit from it.

[2] The word of truth is both the gospel and Scripture. Although some may see these as different things, James does not seem to see any difference between the gospel and the teaching of the whole Bible. He certainly does not see any conflict between 'law' and 'gospel'. He is not dealing with the 'Judaizers' that Paul was facing. Paul was fighting against those who were trusting in the law rather than the Messiah that the law was pointing to. James is fighting against those who talk about trusting in the Father/Jesus but show by their actions that such 'trust' is mere self-deception.

Rather we need to look into the Bible very intently, carefully, diligently and practically. The word of God is not a philosophical theory to be considered or a clever idea to be fascinated by, but a 'perfect law that gives freedom'. The Bible tells us what to do with our lives.

James calls it a 'perfect' ('*teleios*') law, using the same word that he has used to describe the purpose of our spiritual growth in 1:4. The one who trusts in Jesus becomes perfect through various trials as they practice the perfect law that gives them freedom.[3]

Returning to the theme of self-deception, James asks the person who thinks of himself as 'religious' or 'pious' to examine their speech. If they are **quick** to speak, **slow** to listen and **quick** to be angry (verse 19) they can be sure that whatever religion they have is worthless.

When James looks at the kind of religion that has reality and worth, he does not even mention our speech. Far from speaking angry words, the person who has a genuine relationship with God the Father in Jesus the Saviour is a person who shares the patient and compassionate nature of the Father.

The Father's religion is not a matter of human religion at all, with its robes, rituals, shrines, sacred places, etc. No, the Father is interested in a life transformed by the gospel of His glorious Son (see 2:1), a life that **practically** imitates His own heart and practice. There are many other Scriptures that repeat this truth. No-one can claim to be close to the Father if they do not share His activities.

3. Don't Show Favouritism 2:1–7

When we see the connection between favouritism and practical care throughout the Scriptures[4], we see how James is continuing the theme of chapter 1 here in chapter 2.

Showing partiality to the rich and ignoring the widows and orphans is James' test case of being polluted by the world (1:27–2:1). What kind of 'religion' is practised in our church family? Are the elderly cared for properly? Do they spend all week alone, struggling with their daily needs? Do they have enough heating during the winter? Does anybody help them with their shopping or collecting their pension? What help do we give to the single parents in the fellowship? Do the children of single mums find

[3] What does James mean by 'freedom'? In verse 14 he spoke of the evil desires that drag us away, and in 4:1 he again speaks of these evil desires that battle within us, thwarting us. If **doing** the perfect law will rid us of our filth and evil, then it gives freedom from our evil desires, the evil desires that seek to capture and ruin us. This seems to reflect the theology of Psalm 119:9–11.

[4] See Deuteronomy 10:17–18, Leviticus 19:15.

fathers in the church family? Are the house-bound forgotten? Are the sick visited and loved? Do we share our money with those who don't have enough? Are the financial needs of single parent families shared by the whole church?

We cannot claim to be genuine believers in the glorious Lord Jesus if we continue to be polluted by the prejudices of the world. In verses 2–4 James gives a specific example. If we give more care to the rich, to those that the world would esteem, then we show that we are motivated by evil desires. If we treat the poor, the ones that the world rejects, without the respect and love that Jesus commanded and demonstrated, then we show ourselves to be deceived about our 'religion'. We have been dragged away and enticed by evil desires (1:14), failing the testing of our faith.

4. The Law That Gives Freedom 2:8–13

In verse 8 James takes us directly back to the teaching of Jesus once more. Jesus isolated one particular law as being at the very heart of every law governing our behaviour towards each other. Look at Matthew 22:34–40. 'Love the Lord your God with all your heart and with all your soul and with all your mind. This is the first and greatest commandment. And the second is like it: love your neighbour as yourself. All the law and the prophets hang on these two commandments' (verses 37–40).

This law strikes right at the heart of favouritism. If we treat others with the same attention and care that we give to ourselves then we will show no favouritism. Favouritism is sinful. It is sinful because it breaks the law.[5]

Jesus forbids any compartmentalising of the law, see for example Matthew 5:19–22. He exposes the hypocrisy of ignoring what we might consider to be 'the least of these commandments' whilst congratulating ourselves on keeping the commandments that fit in with our lifestyle. James makes the same point. The law is not for picking and choosing. It stands as an interconnected whole, describing the full picture of gospel living. If we reject one aspect of this picture then we reject the lot.

James knows that the Church is no longer under the law, and yet he tells us in verse 12 to 'speak and act as those who are going to be judged by the law that gives freedom'. It is as if he is saying 'for those who believe

[5] James does not need to get into the intricate descriptions of the place and function of the law that Paul does. The law of Moses was given to describe the behaviour of the those who were waiting for the promised Messiah. Even now that the law no longer directly governs the life of the Church, the law still shows us what righteous living looks like. We see many examples of this in the writings of Paul, James, Peter and John.

in Jesus the law shows us how to behave in order to be free of our evil desires. We should speak and act knowing that even as believers we will be judged for how we have lived' (See 2 Corinthians 5:10).

Paul, James and the Law

Some people have felt that Paul and James disagree about the law. Paul is portrayed as attacking the law as a law of bondage and death. James sees the law as a law of liberty. However, we must never caricature Paul. In Romans 2:13 Paul also says that only those who obey the law are declared righteous. In Romans 2:20 he says that the law is the embodiment of knowledge and truth. Romans 7:12 says 'the law is holy, and the commandment is holy, righteous and good', verse 14, 'the law is spiritual'. Romans 7:22 'in my inner being I delight in God's law...' So, according to Paul, how can the law be obeyed? Romans 8:4 'the righteous requirements of the law might be fully met in us, who do not live according to the sinful nature but according to the Spirit'. The person who trusts in Jesus has a new nature and by walking according to the Spirit they are able to live out the holy, righteous and good life that the law describes. Paul explains this in concrete terms – Romans 13:8–10 'Let no debt remain outstanding, except the continuing debt to love one another, for **he who loves his fellow-man has fulfilled the law**. The commandments, 'do not commit adultery', 'do not murder', 'do not steal', 'do not covet', and whatever other commandment there may be, are summed up in this one rule: 'love your neighbour as yourself'. Love does no harm to its neighbour. Therefore love is the fulfilment of the law'. Paul's argument is never with the law itself, but with the abuse of the law that he encountered in those who trusted in the law rather than in the Messiah of the law. To trust in the law for righteousness is to be in bondage and death. To trust in Jesus for righteousness is to be set free to fulfil the law in the power of the Spirit. Paul also refers us to the law to see how we should live our lives, e.g. 1 Corinthians 9:9. The law is a wonderful, prophetic shadow of the glorious life of the kingdom. If we oppose the law we oppose the gospel. If we trust in Jesus and obey His commands, then we fulfil all that the law ever dreamed.[6]

Verse 13 contains a warning – if we show no mercy then we will receive no mercy on the Day of Judgement. This is exactly what Jesus taught in Matthew 18:21–35. James told us that we must not hold faith in Jesus with

[6] See the Galatians Book by Book Study Guide for a deeper analysis of these issues.

favouritism (2:1). Trusting Jesus is totally incompatible with favouritism. James is still making the same point. If we are unmerciful in our relationships we show that we do not really trust in Jesus. If we live in the realm of judgement, then we will receive judgement. If we live in the realm of mercy, then we will receive mercy. The people of Jesus' kingdom show mercy and for them mercy will triumph over the judgement of the last day.

Further Questions

1. How is favouritism actually a denial of the gospel?

2. What was the point of the Old Testament law? Can you think through why the Church is no longer under the law? What is the benefit of studying the law for us now? How did it delight the heart of the Psalmist?

3. What kind of judgment will Christians receive on Judgment Day?

Session 3

James 2:14–26
Faith Without Works is Dead

Key Truth: Real, living faith in Jesus produces fruit and is shown by our actions.

Jesus' teaching:
Matthew 7:16–24 'Do people pick grapes from thorn bushes, or figs from thistles? Likewise every good tree bears good fruit, but a bad tree bears bad fruit. A good tree cannot bear bad fruit, and a bad tree cannot bear good fruit. Every tree that does not bear good fruit is cut down and thrown into the fire. Thus, by their fruit you will recognize them.'
See also Matthew 5:16–20, Matthew 23:23–26

1. Faith by Itself is Dead 2:14–19

James has made it very clear to us, as did Jesus, that we will all be judged according to what we have done, according to the fruit that our lives have produced. If we are good trees then we will produce good fruit, but if we are bad trees then we will produce only bad fruit (Matthew 7:17–29). Jesus' parable of the sheep and the goats is a very clear form of this teaching (Matthew 25:31–46). Jesus, the Son of Man, judges between the sheep and the goats according to the way they lived their lives.

James knows that the gospel is all about **trusting** Jesus. However, he sees that many people are deceiving themselves. They think that they are trusting Jesus, but their lives demonstrate that they are still caught in the unfruitfulness of unbelief. The opposite problem to the legalism that Paul fights against is the 'faithism' that afflicts so much of the Church around the world today. We find this kind of 'faithism' when people speak about accepting Jesus as Saviour but not as Lord. They speak as if they could 'trust' in Jesus for salvation whilst following their own evil desires. On the other hand, we find people who attend Church, say their prayers, avoid gross sins and 'believe' the Bible… yet they have no real relationship with Jesus. Their lives bear no genuine spiritual fruit. They are not people of love, compassion and mercy. James wants us all to know that **real faith issues in real fruit**, heartfelt mercy and practical goodness. If we think we have faith but feel that we are exempt from the kingdom life that Jesus described in Matthew chapters 5–7, then we deceive ourselves. If that is where we are, we need to face up to the fact that we are not trusting in Jesus in the way that the Living God demands.

James perhaps shocked us with his stark statement of the necessity of mercy if we are to receive mercy on the day of judgement. Now, in verse 14, he pushes forward with the same line of thought. Anyone who claims to trust in Jesus but produces none of the good fruit of life in Jesus must face the fact that whatever kind of faith he has is not the kind of faith that can save him.

In verses 15–16 James gives a concrete example of the kind of mercy and good works that he has in mind. He describes a situation where a member of the Church family is suffering in poverty, without food or clothing. The genuine believer will obviously share what they have, or take them to the shops for food and clothing right away. They will behave just like the believers in Acts 2:42–47. However, if a person does nothing more than piously wishing them well, perhaps just offering a prayer for them, it is obvious that they are not a person who has been born again by the word of truth in Jesus. What good are empty words when practical help is required? Such unmerciful behaviour shows a man to be condemned.

The concluding statement of verse 17 couldn't be clearer: 'faith by itself, if it is not accompanied by action, is dead.' A faith that is not matched by a life bearing the fruit of useful mercy and practical compassion is a faith that is **dead**.

Many people know that the great 16th Century reformer, Martin Luther, struggled with the book of James as he sought to proclaim the gospel of salvation by **faith**. However, in his preface to Paul's letter to the Romans, Luther gives perhaps the very best expression of what James is saying in all of Christian literature. It seems strange that Luther didn't recognise this in his own study of James:

> "O it is a living, busy, active mighty thing, this faith. It is impossible for it not to be doing good things incessantly. It does not ask whether good works are to be done, but before the question is asked, it has already done them, and is constantly doing them. Whoever does not do such works, however, is an unbeliever. He gropes and looks around for faith and good works, but knows neither what faith is nor what good works are. Yet he talks and talks, with man words, about faith and good works."

In verse 18 James rejects any idea that genuine faith can be separated from 'the obedience that comes from faith'.[7] He seems to imagine an opponent who says 'you have faith and I have works'. Perhaps we expected him to imagine the opposite objection: 'I have faith, you have works'. However, James would be no happier with a person who took shelter in their works alone. Faith and works must always go together. James' challenge cuts to the heart of the issue: faith can be shown through works, but it can never be shown without works.

James anticipates a further objection. Surely believing in God must show that a person is on the right track? Surely anybody who believes that there is one God must be saved? This is a very common line of thinking in our modern world. People speak as if Islam, Christianity and Judaism are all basically the same because they all share a belief in one God... whatever that God might be. James may well have Deuteronomy 6:4 in mind. Many people regard the confession of this verse to be the most important aspect of Old Testament faith. James rejects this kind of thinking as sharply as he possibly can. A person might confidently say, 'I believe in one God'. James replies, 'well, whoop-di-do! So does the devil.' The only real question is: are you related to the Father through the Son in the power of the Spirit? Do you live out the life of the Living God as you put His Word into practice? Are you **practically** trusting Jesus, the only point of contact between God and humanity?

We must not give anybody credit for mere belief in God. If even the demons fearfully share this belief then there is no value in it whatsoever, unless it is accompanied with the obedience that flows from genuine faith. Whether a person is a monotheist, an atheist or a polytheist makes no difference. They will be judged with no mercy unless they obediently trust in our glorious Lord Jesus Christ, the only One Who can bring us into the fruitful life of God.

2. Abraham's Faith and Works 2:20–23

Like the apostle Paul, James goes back to Abraham to establish the true view of how salvation works. Abraham is the father of the Christian family, so whatever we find in his experience must be the norm for us all. If we require proof of the unbreakable bond between faith and works then the life of Abraham provides it.

Abraham trusted God and it was credited to him as righteousness back in Genesis 15:6. However, when Abraham was told to sacrifice Isaac in Genesis 22 he obeyed without question. Abraham's faith was shown to be real by his obedience. To obey when faced with such a terribly difficult

[7] Romans 1:5

command can only happen when a person genuinely trusts in the Living God. As James 2:22 puts it, Abraham's faith was inseparable from action, and his faith was tested, approved and completed in his actions. A faith that has no actions is no faith at all.

James goes back to the original verdict of Genesis 15 and says that the verdict of righteousness given to Abraham back then was fulfilled or demonstrated by the actions that Abraham's faith produced. He was called God's friend because his faith was no empty 'religion' or barren knowledge (like the demons have). No, Abraham shows how genuine trust will necessarily lead to fruitful obedience.

3. Not by Faith Alone 2:24-26

In verse 24 James gives us a key conclusion. A faith that is separated from fruit and obedience is not the faith that justifies. A faith in Jesus that refuses to follow Him is not a faith that unites us to the death and resurrection of Jesus. James is not telling us that we need to earn our justification, but that God will freely justify only those whose faith in Jesus is a genuine one that produces actions and fruit.

Paul and James on Justification

If we compare Romans 3:28 with James 2:24 we can see why many have discussed how these two Scripture writers are to be related.

Romans 3:28 'we maintain that a man is justified by faith apart from observing the law.'

James 2:24 'You see that a person is justified by what he does and not by faith alone.'

When James says 'faith alone' he is talking about a false faith that produces no fruit. He is certainly not rejecting genuine trust in Jesus alone. When Paul speaks of faith without works of law he is speaking of a faith that trusts in Jesus rather than the law. He certainly does not approve of an inactive faith. We must allow each Biblical writer to mean what they intend to say.

Term	James	Paul
Faith alone	The kind of barren and empty faith that the demons have. A false faith that is shown up by its lack of fruit.	A genuine faith in Jesus that rejects any kind of human boasting before God. A fruitful faith that understands the true purpose of the law.

The example of Rahab is another key one (verse 25). James probably chooses Rahab because she was a Gentile prostitute. In choosing Abraham he chose someone the 'religious' people would find acceptable, but in choosing Rahab he chooses someone who cuts right across their empty piety. Joshua chapter 2 records how faith and action went together in the life of Rahab. In Joshua 2:9–13 we see Rahab making a wonderful confession of faith in the LORD God of Israel. She demonstrated the reality of her faith when she put her life on the line for the sake of the Israelite spies.

The Scriptures are packed full of such examples. Hebrews 11 provides a summary of so many of these saints whose faith in the promised Messiah produced actions and faithfulness.

Verse 26 provides a striking conclusion. A **living** faith is a faith that produces the actions that the Scriptures command. A **dead** faith is a one that claims to trust in Jesus but not enough to actually follow Him in action. A faith without works is like a corpse. It would be ridiculous to declare such a corpse to be a perfectly healthy person. In just that way, it is ridiculous and dangerous for anyone to think of their faith as real or saving if it has no action, no fruit, no spiritual life.

Further Questions

1. Form a succinct answer to someone who says that James and the apostle Paul disagree about justification by faith.

2. Look at Genesis chapter 22. In what ways does the near-sacrifice of Isaac remind us of Jesus going to the Cross? What similarities are there? Why do you think that is? Look at where Isaac and Abraham were at the time – compare Genesis 22:2 with 2 Chronicles 3:1. Why are we given this detail?

Session 4

James 3:1–17
No Man Can Tame the Tongue

Key Truth: The tongue is a powerful and dangerous part of the body. What we say and what we do reveals whether we possess the true wisdom that comes from the Father.

Jesus' teaching:
Matthew 12:33–37 'Make a tree good and its fruit will be good, or make a tree bad and its fruit will be bad, for a tree is recognized by its fruit. You brood of vipers, how can you who are evil say anything good? For out of the overflow of the heart the mouth speaks... But I tell you that men will have to give account on the Day of Judgment for every careless word they have spoken. For by your words you will be acquitted, and by your words you will be condemned.'
See also Matthew 7:16–21, Matthew 15:8–20

1. A Warning to Teachers 3:1–8

James wants to discourage the members of a local church from too readily becoming one of the teachers. The teacher will receive a 'stricter' judgement. This doesn't mean that they will suffer greater punishment, but that they will be examined more closely. The speech of the Bible teacher can have such deep effect and it is absolutely vital that the teacher has control of their tongue.

Controlling the tongue is hard for the teacher because **everybody** stumbles, especially in what we say (verse 2). James began his letter by showing us that the goal of our spiritual growth is perfection or maturity. Now he tells us that the Christian who has control over their speech is perfect. In other words, if we want to reach full maturity in Jesus we must make our speech the top priority.

In verses 3–8 James piles on the imagery to demonstrate the power of the tongue and the importance of controlling it. We may think of words as 'only words'. We might think that words can be easily undone, that we don't always say what we mean, that our actions are more important than our words. James is pleading with us to radically revise our understanding of our speech. If we remember the role of speech in the Living God we begin to see the power of words. The Word of the Father is Jesus Who accomplishes everything that the Father wills. The universe was created as the Father spoke His Word.

Up to verse 5, James has shown us the great power of the tongue, but now he instructs us about the great evil that lies in the tongue. He points us to the incredibly destructive power of a tiny spark in a forest. The spark may seem tiny, yet it can burn down hundreds of trees.

The tongue is also a fire and it gets its fire from hell, verse 6. Some think of hell as the headquarters of evil and that hell exercises its evil influence over the tongue. However, Jesus defines hell as the place of **punishment** for evil. Hell is the very last place that the armies of evil want to be. It will, of course, actually be the very last place they will be for all eternity. Therefore, it is more likely that James is saying the tongue brings judgement on humanity. It is as if the tongue is already in its place of punishment, already tasting the judgement that awaits it. Whatever is the case, the fire of the tongue sets fire to 'the whole person' not just at one time but for the whole of their life on earth. The evil power of the tongue cannot be contained or limited.

However, in verses 7–8 James gives us more bad news! The tongue is far more difficult to control than wild animals. As nervous as we might be in the presence of a 'domesticated' tiger, we should be far more nervous of even the most disciplined tongue! Returning to the pessimism of verse 2, James tells us bluntly that no man can control the tongue. It is wilder than the wildest animal. It is a restless evil beast with an extremely poisonous bite. We need to pray to our generous Father for help. We will see from verse 13 that the wisdom that He gives us can help us even against the ravenous evil of our speech.

2. Out of the Same Mouth 3:9–12

In 1:8 James condemned double-mindedness and now he condemns double-speaking: blessing and cursing with the same mouth. He confronts us with the impossible contradiction of using our tongue both to praise 'our Lord and Father' as well as cursing humans who are in the image of the Father, Son and Holy Spirit.[8] If we curse somebody (as Jesus taught in Matthew 5:21–22) we murder them. In Genesis 9:6 we see the connection between murder and the image of God – 'whoever sheds the blood of man, by man shall his blood be shed; for in the image of God has God made man'. Cursing a human being is an attack on the Living God. **What possible value can our 'praising' be if it comes from a heart that is happy to curse the image of God?**

James reaches into the origin of such a contradiction. In chapter 1 the heart that wobbles between doubt and faith is actually revealed to be actually a heart of doubt alone. Here, in the same way, a tongue that produces both cursing and blessing actually reveals a corrupt heart of unbelief. Remember Matthew 12:33–34 quoted above.

3. Who is Wise among You? 3:13–17

Now James returns to the specific question of teachers. He challenges the potential teachers as to whether they think they have wisdom and understanding. Just as faith must be shown in action, so must wisdom and understanding. This seems to be based on Jesus' words in Matthew 11:19 'wisdom is proved right by her actions'.

The key feature of the wise person here is **humility** (verse 13). What a challenge this is to the teacher! When we look at the Academy, the teaching staff at a university, humility is usually the very last thing we ever find. In the Church the very opposite must be found. The Bible teacher must be a person who has demonstrated that they have real wisdom and understanding by their humility and good fruit.

In many situations I have been asked to sign doctrinal statements to check my orthodoxy, but I have very rarely been asked about the way I put the truth into practice. So often theological training is focussed on the accumulation of knowledge, but the development of wisdom and understanding is largely ignored. This needs to be taken seriously.

In verse 14 we see that arrogance and pride is actually a denial of the truth. When we find selfish ambition in our hearts we mustn't give it any room at all. It is one of the evil desires that will drag us into temptation, sin and death. A leading minister commented that **envy** lurks behind many of the problems in evangelical unity (see verse 16). How can a teacher train the Church family to maturity/perfection if they are motivated by envy and pride?

The contrast between the two kinds of wisdom is common in the Bible. In the book of Proverbs it is the straightforward contrast between wisdom

---

[8] This is the only time in the Bible that the Father is referred to as 'Lord and Father'.

and folly. In 1 Corinthians 1:18–2:16 Paul makes one of the longest explanations of these two 'wisdoms' – the wisdom of God stands in total opposition to the wisdom of man. James goes even further. The wisdom of man that produces the fruit of envy, pride and selfish ambition is from the devil. Far from being the wisdom given by the Father above (James 1:5), it is given by the devil below. James wants us to recoil in horror at such wisdom. Pride, envy and selfish ambition are not understandable failings: they are the work of demonic power corrupting and destroying the Church family.

These are sobering words! We cannot have a neutral wisdom. We are either asking and receiving our wisdom from the Father or we are being infiltrated and subverted by the wisdom of the devil. We can tell which wisdom controls a person by examining their humility and practical mercy.

To further assist our recognition of the Father's wisdom James gives us a careful description in verse 17.

Pure	**First of all**... Purity stands in absolute opposition to the devil and the evil desires of the human heart.
Peace-loving	Controversy and argument is tragically a common feature of Church life. This is a terrible evil. It is a sign that we do not have the wisdom of the Father. No end of arguments are excused with the words 'we must defend the truth', but what kind of truth are we defending when it brings us into such bitter dispute with our brothers and sisters in Christ?
Considerate	Thinking of the needs of others before our own.
Submissive	Matthew 20:25–27 'You know that the rulers of the Gentiles lord it over them, and their high officials exercise authority over them. Not so with you. Instead, whoever wants to become great among you must be your servant, and whoever wants to be first must be your slave...'
Full of mercy	James has already told us that mercy is an essential product of our faith. The Father's wisdom produces practical help for the Church family.
Full of good fruit	A good tree produces good fruit. It is impossible for it not to, according to Jesus. When we want to know how 'orthodox' a Christian is we need to look for good fruit more than their willingness to sign a statement of faith.[9]
Impartial	James has thoroughly shown this to us. The faith of our glorious Lord Jesus is totally incompatible with favouritism.
Sincere	A person might be able to make an outward show of true wisdom for a time, but there will be no sincerity about their actions. Sincerity shows that what we do and say come from the heart, from what we really are.

[9] This is not to say that heresy is unimportant so long as a person produces good fruit.

Further Questions

1. Why is controlling our speech so important? Consider what the Bible has to say about the speech of the Lord. Look at Psalms 29 and 33, and think where else in the Bible each member of the Trinity speaks.

2. James sees wisdom and understanding in the same way as he sees faith. Why? The book of Proverbs begins with David instructing Solomon in the importance of Wisdom. Wisdom is a **Person**. Make a list of all the things that are said about Wisdom in those first 9 chapters (e.g. Proverbs 3:13–20; 4:5–9; **8:22–31**). Who do you think Wisdom is? At this stage do not worry about the fact that Wisdom is a woman. The Holy Spirit is also always feminine in the Hebrew Scriptures. Who is the Craftsman of creation? Who can give us the grace and favour of the Living God? Who is worth more than all the treasure in the world?

Session 5

James 3:18–4:17 Humble Yourselves before the Lord

Key Truth: As the bride of Christ, the Church seeks to humbly and faithfully commit to Jesus. We give up our selfish and envious desires to promote peace, not quarrels in the Church family.

Jesus' teaching:
Luke 14:11 'For everyone who exalts himself will be humbled, and he who humbles himself will be exalted.'
See also Matthew 5:1–9, Matthew 11:29, Matthew 5:21–24, Luke 18:9–14

1. Peace and Strife 3:18–4:3

In James 1:20, we saw that human anger does not achieve God's righteousness. The reverse is also true: in peace wisdom can flourish.

Why are there so many fights and arguments in the Church family (4:1)? Such division is never produced by the Father's wisdom, but by the evil desires of the human heart. These evil desires make war against our very soul (see 1 Peter 2:11). We have seen this theme throughout James. The mature (Greek: '*teleios*') church has thrown out the evil desires by **doing** the word of truth, taught by the teachers who have shown their wisdom and understanding in humility and action. The church that is wracked by arguments and strife shows itself to be immature and still controlled by evil desires and the devil's wisdom.

What we should do is ask our generous Father for all that we need. Fighting for our own interests and agendas reveals that we do not have confidence in our Father to supply our real needs.

In these verses, James helps us understand the issue of 'unanswered prayers' – or rather, not getting our own way in prayer. He seems to say that we will **always** receive what we ask for if our prayers are asked in the Father's wisdom. As long as our prayers are directed by the devil's wisdom, motivated by selfish and personal agendas, our prayers will be ignored by the Father. If we want our prayers to be effective then we must become mature. James will return to this issue of prayer at the end of chapter 5.

2. God versus the World and the Devil 4:4–10

James' affectionate 'dear brothers' is replaced now with a much more confrontational address: 'you adulterous people' (verse 4).

We see this same kind of language in Isaiah 57, the book of Hosea, and throughout the Scriptures (see for example Jeremiah 3:6–10). James takes up this language and directs it at the reader. If we want the affection of the world we are committing adultery against our true Husband, Jesus Christ. James pulls the respectable veneer off our worldliness and exposes it for what it really is. The Church should love her divine Husband with total faithfulness and devotion. The very fact that we might want the affection of the world reveals the adultery in our hearts.

We seek the affection of the world when we keep silent about Jesus at work or in our neighbourhood. We seek the friendship of the world when we store up treasures on earth instead of using our resources to look after and equip the Christian family. We commit adultery when we try to fit in with the values and lifestyle of the world rather than Jesus. We betray our divine Fiancé when we are not satisfied with His love and find our fulfilment in this passing world.

To go after a lover when we are betrothed to Jesus is a terrible evil and makes us into His enemy. How heart-broken a husband is when his wife or fiancé runs off with another man! This gives us a glimpse into the much greater and deeper betrayal when the Church prefers the love of the world to the love of Jesus. The Father, Son and Holy Spirit are not willing to share the Church with the world. We might normally think of jealousy or envy as simply sinful. When we are jealous or envious for what does not belong to us then it is sinful. However, if we are jealous for what is ours then it is right and proper.

Even in our adultery, Jesus reaches out to draw us back to Himself. Verse 6 tells us that He does not divorce us but offers us more grace, more affection, so that we can turn away from loving the affection of the world. James reminds us of Proverbs 3:34. The proud are those who seek the friendship of the world. However, if we are humble Jesus will give us more love, more strength, more affection, more **grace**.

So, we are faced with a clear, stark choice (verse 7): Jesus or the world; God or the devil. James is simply stripping away confusion, compromise and pretence to let us see reality as it really is. Behind all our sophisticated selfish agendas and sinful actions stands the devil. There are only two directions to go in: towards the devil or towards God. Yes, the devil with all his power and resources cannot overpower the bride of Christ if she submits herself to her Husband.

Verses 8–10 are wonderful verses of a fresh beginning. We don't need to remain in spiritual adultery one second longer. Right now we can repent, resist the devil and come near to Jesus in humility and sorrow for our sin. We do not need to be double-minded any longer. Our spiritual unfaithfulness should cause us deep heartache, shame and pain. The wonderful truth experienced by all His children is that the Father will forgive us and restore us with such love and warmth. He holds no grudges or bitterness. He forgets our sins and will never call them back to memory.

3. All Such Boasting is Evil 4:11–17

Now James returns to the matter of the division and fighting within the Church family. It seems that James has shown us the root cause of waging war on each other – it comes from our evil desires. We are controlled by our evil desires because we prefer the friendship of the world to the love of Jesus.

Now James gives us further diagnosis. The general problem that James examines is slander within the Church. Jesus told us in Matthew 7:1 not to judge each other. Passing judgement on each other comes from arrogance and pride. The remedy for this is the humility that we find in drawing near to God.

The law that James speaks of in verse 11 might well be Jesus' command from Matthew 7:1. If we go ahead and judge our fellow Christians then we have taken a position above the commands of Jesus. To judge the law of Jesus as being irrelevant to our own situation is to take His place as the one Lawgiver and Judge (verse 12). Jesus alone is the One Who is able to save us or condemn us. The only attitude we are allowed to take towards Him is humility, trust and obedience. The moment we pick and choose which of His commands we want to follow we have proclaimed ourselves as Lord and Saviour.

This problem of arrogance and pride is also revealed in the way we think about our future plans (verses 13–16). The humble and mature believer never forgets that their future lies entirely in the hands of our

Heavenly Father. Every day we must cast ourselves wholeheartedly on the providence and care of our Father in heaven. We must never take even a single day for granted.

James does not want us simply to add the words 'God willing' to every statement of purpose (although that might have its use). It is more that we live each day and make our plans in full and humble submission to the Father, Son and Holy Spirit.

Further Questions

1. In what ways does marriage reflect the relationship between Jesus and His bride, the Church? What will it mean to be married to Jesus after His return?

2. Thinking of verses 13–17, what else does the Bible have to say about planning our future? How does the Lord guide us? What do we already know is the Lord's 'will' for each of our lives?

Session 6

James 5:1–20
The Judge is Standing at the Door

Key Truth: The glories of our future with Jesus will far outweigh all the sufferings of our present lives.

Jesus' teaching:
Matthew 6:19–21 'Do not store up for yourselves treasures on earth, where moth and rust destroy, and where thieves break in and steal. But store up for yourselves treasures in heaven, where moth and rust do not destroy, and where thieves do not break in and steal. For where your treasure is, there your heart will be also.'
See also Luke 6:20–26, Matthew 6:24–34, Matthew 5:39, Matthew 5:33–37

1. Weep and Wail You Rich People 5:1–6

The final chapter of James makes hard reading for most Western Christians. In comparison to the vast majority of Christians around the world, Western Christians are very rich. Most of us might think of ourselves as merely 'comfortable' rather than rich, but we need to compare ourselves to the poor of the world rather than the other rich people in Western society. The very fact that being overweight is considered to be one of the great problems of Western society reveals the truth. Why do we keep so many things for ourselves? It is very sobering to discover how much money a family lives on in different parts of the world.

Jesus tells the rich man in Matthew 19:21–27 to sell what he has and give to the poor. Although we might want to quickly dismiss the possibility of applying this to ourselves, when we read Acts 2:42–47 we see that the Post-Pentecost Church did in fact sell their riches as the Church family had need. The idea that there would be people in poverty in the Church family whilst others in the family were rich is almost unthinkable in the light of these Scriptures.

In verse 1 James does not specify whether he is talking about believers or unbelievers. However, as he goes in it seems clear that anyone who trusts in wealth is **not** a genuine believer. Storing up treasure on earth is a clear example of seeking the friendship of the world.

Recalling Jesus' teaching of Matthew 6:20, James points out how all earthly treasure is decaying and rotting (verse 3). The very fact that gold and silver items need frequent polishing to maintain their look cry out that such treasure is **passing away**. James is particularly outraged that this hoarding up of earthly treasures happens **in the last days**. Now that we stand on the very brink of Judgement Day, it is even more wilfully evil to invest in this passing age.

In verse 4 James points to our economic practices. Who suffers so that we can enjoy our wealth? Do workers have to work on low wages so that we can enjoy our earthly treasures? Where does our food come from? Are there farmers struggling to survive because of the economic systems that give us the quantity, quality and variety of food that we like?[10] Is our Christian family a shining example of Jesus' answers to the world's problems? Is the use and distribution of money in our fellowship a bright light displaying the power and effect of the gospel?

2. The Lord is Coming 5:7–12

The person who has a living, active faith in Jesus lives with their heart always fixed on His coming. We are pilgrims now, we are aliens waiting for our true home, the renewal of the whole creation. The farmer invests in the future, waiting patiently for the Lord's provision of rain so that he can harvest his valuable crop. That is how we must be (verses 7–8), patiently waiting for the truly valuable treasure of His kingdom that will expose all earthly treasure for what it is.

The return of Jesus might seem to be taking a long time, but just as our lives are like a quickly vanishing mist, so the Lord's coming is near. In a very short time we will be gathered together at the marriage feast of Jesus. We cannot think about this too much. Every day we should remind ourselves of this marvellous future that is so very near.

Rather than grumbling at each other we need to be patient in our sufferings (verse 10). We are back to the place where the letter began – thinking about how to endure our many trials.

---

[10] Traidcraft is a Christian organisation that seeks to give fair prices to poor workers around the world. You can find out more about them from their website: www.traidcraft.co.uk The Fairtrade organisation tries to make sure that farmers receive a fair price for their crops and many Fairtrade items can be found at regular supermarkets. Find out more at: www.fairtrade.org.uk

James picks Job for special mention. Why? Because Job gives us a full picture of how our sufferings are not forever. Job refused to doubt the LORD God throughout his sufferings, yet the book of Job ends with him receiving amazing blessings. Job teaches us that at the end, at the coming of the Lord Jesus, we will receive blessings that will infinitely outweigh any of the sufferings that we have faced in this brief life. We see the same pattern of faithful, obedient perseverance in the lives of Moses, Abraham, David, Elijah, Jeremiah, Ezekiel, Hosea, John the Baptist, etc.

James seems to reach a crescendo in verse 17 – '**above all**, my brothers, do not swear…' How does this connect with patient perseverance? James is clearly quoting Jesus' teaching of Matthew 5:33–37. If we are suffering for the name of Jesus, we might well be tempted to be economical with the truth. Straight talking may well bring us more suffering when people are set against us. However, we must never fall into this trap. We must always speak the simple truth.

3. Praying in Faith 5:13–20

Prayer is the great theme of the letter's conclusion. The letter began by telling us to ask from our generous Father and that is how it ends. Prayer that comes from a humble and trusting heart is the answer to so many of the problems that James has addressed.

There is a good balance in this verse. Some of us stop praying when we are happy, only 'remembering' our prayers when we are in a mess. Others of us stop praying when we are in trouble, allowing doubts and fears to cloud our relationship with the Father. James puts us all right. Whether we are in sorrow or joy, trouble or comfort, good times or bad, we should pour out our hearts to our heavenly Father who loves us so deeply.

Finally, James addresses the time of sickness. What should we do then? Well, we should pray, but this time our prayers should be shared with the elders of our local church.

Verses 14–16 have provoked a great deal of controversy over the years. Is James promising that after the elders have prayed and anointed the sick person they will be restored to full health?

The translation of verse 15 is at the heart of the matter. The most literal translation is something like this: 'and the prayer of faith will **save** the sick person and the Lord will raise him up and if he has committed sins, they will be forgiven'. Now, given that James has spoken so much about the way we must patiently, trustingly persevere in our trials, it does not seem likely that they will be simply taken away as soon as we pray about them. The apostle Paul seemed to have some kind of eye trouble and he was never healed of the disease.

From what we have learned from James we know that his great concern for a person in their illness would be that they are true to Jesus Christ. James has just been setting our gaze very firmly on the imminent return of Jesus. Therefore it seems probable that the sense of verse 15 is that the sick person must continue to pray with genuine faith, knowing that such faith in Jesus will result in our salvation and resurrection **when Jesus returns**. This fits well with the example of verse 11, where we are to patiently wait for what the Lord will **finally** bring about. This also explains the end of verse 15. Forgiveness of sin is promised, and that is the very greatest comfort of all as we face our death.

Now, what about verse 14? Anointing with oil is a practice from the Hebrew Scriptures. Throughout the Bible this anointing with oil not only indicates consecration but also the presence of the Spirit.[11]

So, the sick person is to be anointed with oil by the local church leaders. If we follow this Old Testament teaching, this anointing must be to dedicate the person and to indicate to them the presence of the Spirit to sustain and strengthen them. They are going through a difficult time, yet they are being dedicated to the Lord's service even when they might be confined to bed. It is a time when they can experience spiritual growth. The suffering is almost 'claimed' for the Lord's service. On top of that, the Lord will give them all that they need to go through their suffering with faith, humility and even joy (1:2). None of this is to say that the person may not be miraculously healed by the Lord, but it reminds us that our sufferings are to be claimed as trials that will test our faith and bring us to maturity/perfection.

But, verse 16, it is not just the sick person who needs to deal with their sin. The whole Church family needs to confess their sins to each other and pray for each other so that you (plural) may be healed. Well, what 'healing' does the Church family need? If we go back to 4:1 we see straight away. The church that has allowed sin to fester and grow is a church 'at each others' throats'. The way to healing for such a fellowship is the confession of sin to each other and prayer for each other.

It seems clear that James has the thoughts of chapter 4:1–3 in mind because of the end of verse 16. In 4:1–3 he told us why our prayers are ineffective. Now he tells us the secret of effective prayer. We have seen the connection between wisdom, maturity and righteousness through the letter. Now James pulls it together. The righteous man – the man who is wise and mature, merciful and humble, showing his faith in action – has

[11] In Zechariah 4, when the prophet asks for an explanation of the ever-burning oil lamps, he is told that they represent the power of the Spirit. We also see this very clearly when David was anointed with oil to be king of Israel in 1 Samuel 16:13

the ear of the Father. Such a person does not pray selfishly or sinfully. Their prayers are in harmony with the heart and mind of the Father. The prayers of such a Christian will always be granted.

The secret of powerful and effective prayer is not found in any special techniques or programmes. It is found in drawing near to the Living God. It is not that we will **earn** the answers to our prayers, but that we will be set free from the evil desires that cause us to ask wrongly.

In verses 17–18 James gives us a great example of this kind of prayer. Elijah had a radical impact on national and international events through his prayers. This is a man who had become mature, whose trust in the Lord was tested and refined. Examine the life of Elijah. He is so completely given over to the LORD God. Yet, says James, verse 11, there was nothing special about Elijah as such. He was just the same as every other Christian believer. There is no reason that we too can't pray like Elijah… if we are as zealous for Jesus as he was (I Kings 19:10).

James ends his letter by telling us what Jesus set out in Matthew chapter 18. If any member of the Church family falls into sin we must do all that we can to bring them back. We must forget ourselves and pray, act and speak only for the good of that wandering brother or sister. The remedy for all people who fall into sin is the same – to be brought back to repentance and to a living faith in Christ Jesus.

Further Questions

1. What does James say about healing, 5:14–15? How many kinds of 'healing' is he talking about? We know that the Lord sometimes heals people who are ill, but this does not always happen. When will the promised healing of every illness take place? (Revelation 21:1–4) How is the Lord working towards that time even now?

2. Look at how the Bible tells us we should deal with a Christian who sins unrepentantly. Matthew 18:15–20, 1 Corinthians 5:9–13. Do you think this is a harsh treatment? Why do you think the Bible commands such action in these circumstances? How often do we follow this practice in our own church?.